Totems,
Decoys,
and
Covered
Wagons

JEREMY COMINS

Totems, Decoys, and Covered Wagons

CARDBOARD CONSTRUCTIONS
FROM
EARLY AMERICAN LIFE

Lothrop, Lee & Shepard Company
A DIVISION OF WILLIAM MORROW & COMPANY, INC.
NEW YORK

Also by Jeremy Comins

Art from Found Objects
Eskimo Crafts and their Cultural Backgrounds
Latin American Crafts and their Cultural Backgrounds

Drawings and photographs by the author
except where noted

Printed in the United States of America.

1   2   3   4   5   80   79   78   77   76

Library of Congress Cataloging in Publication Data

Comins, Jeremy.
    Totems, decoys, and covered wagons.
    SUMMARY: Directions for making large-scale, cardboard replicas of objects representative of American Indian and colonial life, such as houses, furniture, toys, and other artifacts.
    1. Paper work—Juvenile literature. 2. Indian craft—Juvenile literature.
3. United States—History—Colonial period, ca. 1600-1775—Juvenile Literature. [1. Paper work. 2. Indian craft. 3. United States—Social life and customs—Colonial period, ca. 1600-1775. 4. Handicraft] I. Title.
TT870.C62   745.59'2   75-44182
ISBN 0-688-41739-6
ISBN 0-688-51739-0 lib. bdg.

To Eleanor

Acknowledgments

———◄◄•►►———

I wish to thank Harry Comins for helping to establish the basic direction of this book, and Eleanor and Edith Comins for their help in discussing the appropriateness of the material included.

Many thanks to my students at Brooklyn Technical High School who made some of the projects. Photographs of their work are indicated with an (S) after each student's name. All student work was done under the direction of the author.

My thanks also to my son Aaron, who was my right hand while mine was broken.

Many of the photographs were taken at Old Bethpage Village Restoration in Old Bethpage, Long Island, New York. I am grateful for the helpfulness extended to me there.

Contents

Introduction

The lives of early Americans, both Indian and Colonial, were rich in creative art and craft techniques. In this book I have chosen objects from varied cultural groups of early America that can be adapted to simple construction. At the same time I hope to provide an understanding of the importance these objects had in the lives of the early makers, and of their unique decorative and design qualities.

I hope this book will awaken your interest in early American life and will lead you to explore the great variety of objects made by our creative ancestors.

BOTTOM PHOTOGRAPH COURTESY OF MUSEUM OF THE AMERICAN INDIAN, HEYE FOUNDATION.

Constructing With Cardboard

BASIC TOOLS

The following tools will be needed for all of the projects in this book. They can be purchased at hardware stores or lumberyards that have a tool supply section. You may also find them in art supply stores.

MATT KNIFE: Look for one with a retractable blade, which makes the knife more portable and safer.

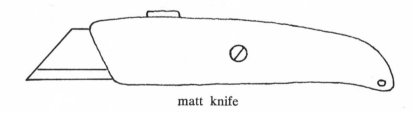

matt knife

X-ACTO KNIFE: Look for the number 1 size with a number 11 blade. This knife is helpful, but you can do without it if need be. It can be found in hobby stores.

I suggest buying an extra package of blades for each knife, as they get dull rather quickly.

#1 X-acto knife with #11 blade

13

CUTTING BOARD: This can be a piece of plywood or homesote. A good size to get is 20 x 24 inches.

MASKING TAPE: A roll of 1½-inch tape is best. Buy it in a building or painting supply store. Artist quality tape is not needed for these projects and is very much more expensive.

24-INCH METAL RULER: This will help you draw straighter lines than you can with a wooden ruler.

ELMER'S OR OTHER WHITE GLUE

PENCIL

ERASER

SMALL SHARP SCISSORS

These comprise your basic tools. Additional tools, if needed, will be listed with each project.

MATERIALS

CARDBOARD: All the projects will be constructed from cardboard boxes, cardboard cylinders, and flat cardboard. Cardboard is made in three basic types:

Type 1: single-thickness cardboard (Figure 1);

Type 2: corrugated cardboard (Figure 2);

Type 3: double-thickness corrugated cardboard (Figure 3); this type is used to package heavy items like furniture.

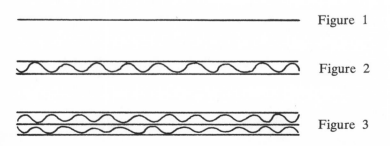

Figure 1

Figure 2

Figure 3

Before starting to work, obtain a few pieces of each type of cardboard to have on hand. Save the sides of cereal or cookie boxes for Type 1. Go to your local stores at the end of the day when boxes are discarded and look for Types 2 and 3. Cut several sheets of each kind with your matt knife.

Also save the cardboard cylinders from packages of aluminum foil, waxed paper, and plastic wrap. I have found that the cardboard cylinders used for paper towels and bathroom tissue are not strong enough.

PAINT: For painting cardboard, you will use water-base and acrylic paints. Water-base paint or household paint can be found in hardware or home decorating stores. Use it when you are painting a whole box or other large surface. A small can will be enough for several projects.

Acrylic paint comes in tubes—you can find it in art and craft supply shops. It is useful when you are painting only a small area or using several colors in a design, since you can buy it in small amounts. One tube will last quite a while.

TECHNIQUES
LAMINATING: In some projects you will need double-thickness corrugated cardboard. If you can't find any, you can make your own by laminating two pieces of single-thickness corrugated cardboard together. You can also

15

build your projects out of single-thickness cardboard instead, without laminating, but they will not be as strong.

To learn how to laminate, try making this laminated square.

1. With your metal ruler and pencil, rule two 10 x 10-inch squares on single-thickness corrugated cardboard. Then place the cardboard on your cutting board. Hold the metal ruler down firmly along one of the lines and with your other hand pull your matt knife along the line. You should be able to cut through the cardboard with one pass of the knife. This will give you a clean sharp edge.

Cut out both squares this way (Figure 4).

2. Spread an even coat of Elmer's glue over one or both squares and press them together (Figure 5).

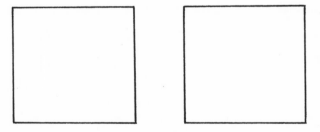

Figure 4

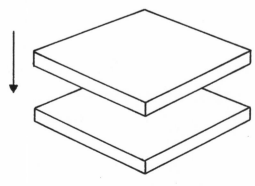

Figure 5

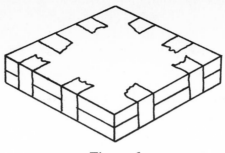

Figure 6

3. Tape the edges together with masking tape (Figure 6). Then put the double cardboard on the kitchen floor or other hard surface with a heavy weight on top of it. (Cover the floor with newspaper to protect it from possible glue seepage.) If you put the weight on without taping the edges, the cardboard pieces will shift position. Let them dry overnight.

Remove the tape slowly so the cardboard's surface doesn't get roughened too much. However, some slight surface tearing is to be expected. Smear some glue into the rough areas with your finger. This will harden the surface.

If you laminate carefully, you will have a strong double-thickness cardboard sheet.

SLOTTING: Slotting two pieces of cardboard will provide a firm joint if the slots are tight. Make a practice slot to see how to do it.

1. Cut one 10-inch square of cardboard as in Figure 4 (page 16).

2. Measure the thickness of the cardboard square. Then draw parallel lines on the square with pencil and ruler;

17

they should be the same distance apart as the thickness
of the cardboard (Figure 7). It is better to make the lines
a little too close together than too far apart; you will be
able to force the cardboard into a tight slot, but it will
not hold if the slot is too loose.
3. With your matt knife, cut along the two parallel lines
(Figure 8). Cut each line with one pass of the knife.

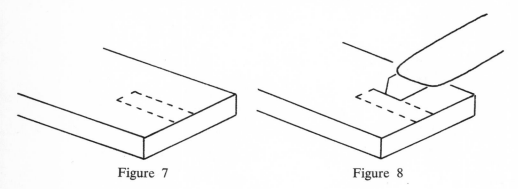

Figure 7   Figure 8

4. With the tip of your X-acto knife, cut across the lines
(Figure 9). Here is where the thin point of the X-acto
knife is very useful. However, with care you can make this
cut with the matt knife.
5. You should now have a clean cut slot (Figure 10).
Slide a piece of the same kind of cardboard into it to test
the fit. If the cardboard moves too easily in the slot, try
again.

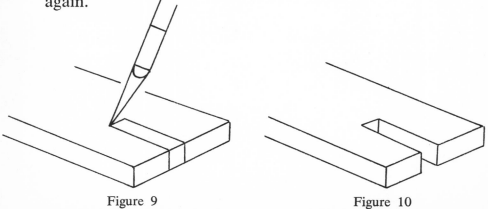

Figure 9   Figure 10

A WORD ABOUT BOXES

Cardboard boxes are made for various purposes, and some are stronger than others. Before selecting a box for your project, check the joints to see if they are firmly attached. Make sure the bottom is strong. You can test this by pressing your hand into the bottom to feel the resistance of the cardboard. Boxes made to hold heavy or expensive items are usually quite strong.

A WORD ABOUT SIZE

Feel free to vary the size and proportions of any of the projects in the book. Often the size of your cardboard construction will be determined by the size of the boxes you find.

The sizes I have indicated for each project are just for your information; they are the sizes of the constructions in the photographs. If you make your construction smaller or larger than the size indicated, you will have to adjust the proportions of all its parts.

A metric conversion chart is supplied on page 120 for use with metric measurements.

You are now ready to start building the constructions.

Haida House

The Haida Indians of the northwest Pacific coast were one of the many tribes that excelled in the construction of wooden houses and the carving of totem poles. A Haida house had one totem pole set in the front and smaller ones on the corners of the roof.

A cardboard Haida house with a door cut in one side

Model of a Haida Indian house.
COURTESY OF THE BROOKLYN MUSEUM.

Cardboard Haida Indian house, 12 inches square and 8 inches high. The totem pole is 13 inches high. MADE BY KENNETH DE GEORGE (S).

can be a dollhouse to use with toy figures or models. Or you might make a smaller Haida house to decorate your room.

Materials
basic tools, *plus*
1 box, about 12 x 12 x 9 inches
singe-thickness corrugated cardboard, about 13 x 20 inches
2 cardboard cylinders from aluminum foil
thin cardboard from a cereal box
water-base paint, gray
acrylic paint, black and white and other bright colors of
   your choice
½-inch paintbrush
#2 pointed watercolor brush

21

How to Make It

1. Place the box in a clear work area (Figure 1).

2. Mark the center of one top edge of the box with a pencil. Then measure down an equal distance from the top at each of the two corners. This distance can be about 2 to 4 inches. The farther down you measure, the steeper the roof's angle will be (Figure 2).

3. Connect the marks with pencil and ruler. Then mark the back of the box the same way and connect the front and back with ruled lines across the sides (Figure 3). Cut along these lines.

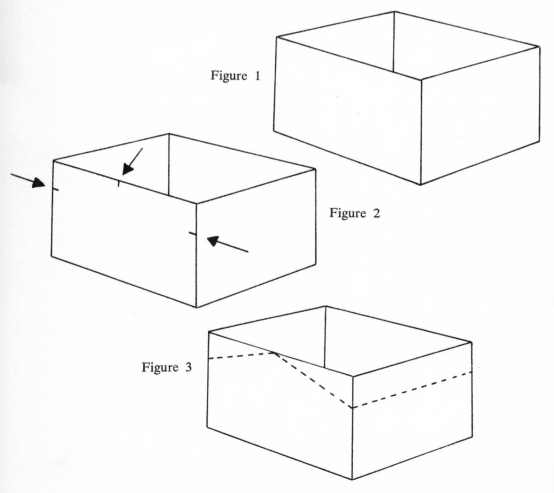

Figure 1

Figure 2

Figure 3

4. Measure the length of the two slanted lines on the front of the box and measure one side edge. Then use ruler and pencil to draw a cardboard rectangle with these measurements for the roof. If you want the roof to extend beyond the walls of the house, make the rectangle a little larger in both directions.

5. Cut out the roof. Draw a line across it at the center. Score this line lightly with the tip of the X-acto knife. Take care not to cut too deeply into the cardboard (Figure 4).

6. Bend the roof on the scored line and glue it to the top edges of the house (Figure 5). Use masking tape to hold the roof in position and let the glue dry overnight.

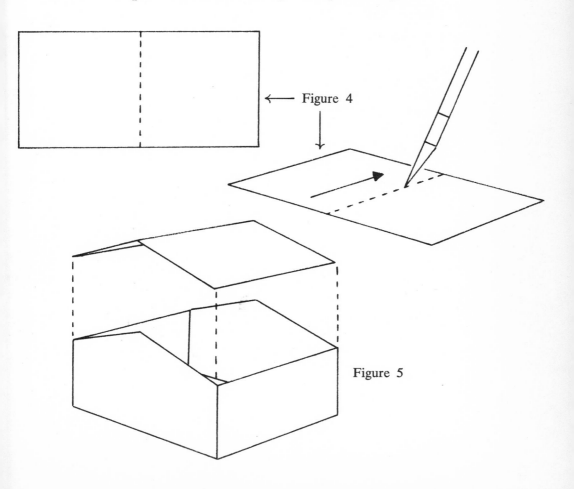

Figure 4

Figure 5

Take the tape off carefully and rub glue into any cardboard surfaces roughened by the removal of the tape.

7. The totem poles are made from the 1½-inch diameter cardboard cylinders (Figure 6). Cut one of the cylinders in half—these shorter cylinders will be the corner totem poles.

8. Trace around the end of one cylinder three times on the cereal-box cardboard. Cut these circles out with a scissors and glue them to the tops of the three cylinders (Figure 7).

9. Glue the tall cylinder to the front of the house. Cut down the shorter ones to the height you want, and then cut the bottoms with a scissors a little bit at a time until they fit the angle of the roof (Figure 8). Glue them to the roof corners.

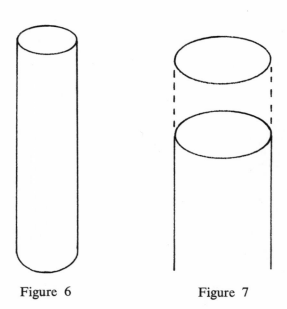

Figure 6   Figure 7

10. You can slot and glue a beak into the top of the main totem pole to make a bird. Cut a thin slot into the cylinder with the X-acto knife and insert a beak cut from thin cardboard (Figure 9). Notice the projection that fits into the slot.

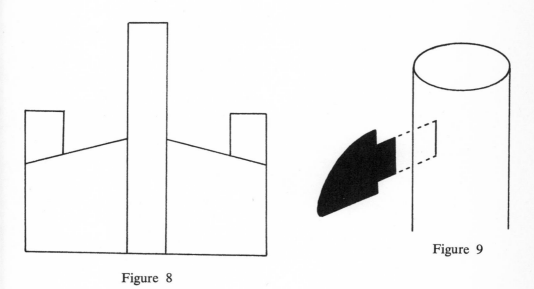

Figure 8

Figure 9

Painting

11. Paint the whole house with gray paint to suggest weathered wood. Two thin coats will look better than one heavy one.

Rule light pencil lines to suggest boards, as in the photo on page 21. Dilute the black acrylic paint with water in a paper cup and paint over the lines with the point of the #2 brush.

25

12. Now sketch the totem pole designs on the cylinders. One possible design is shown in Figure 10. You can modify it or use other photos and drawings in this book for ideas.

13. Paint the main outlines with diluted black acrylic paint. Add colors as you wish to each section. The paint should be mixed with water so it will flow on smoothly and will look opaque and not streaky.

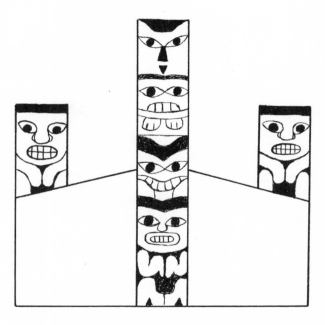

Figure 10

Totem Pole

Totem poles were made by the Indians along the north-west Pacific coast as far as Alaska. They were carved from cedar wood, and some were more than 90 feet high. The poles were often set into the ground facing the water.

The natives of the Northwest Coast still live on their ancestral village site, but in modernized houses. The totem poles still face the waterfront.
PHOTOGRAPH COURTESY OF MUSEUM OF THE AMERICAN INDIAN, HEYE FOUNDATION.

Carved head with a beak. This motif was often used in totem poles.
FROM THE COLLECTION OF ELAINE AND BERNHARD KRAUSS.

Animals, humans, and supernatural creatures were carved on totem poles. It is believed that the figures usually had religious or social significance. However, some of the carving may be purely decorative. The beautiful flowing lines and the expression of the faces and figures establish these unique carvings as masterpieces of art.

Materials
basic tools, *plus*
cardboard box, any size
water-base or acrylic paints or waterproof markers, any
  colors
black construction paper (optional)

28

You can make your totem pole any size, from a desk-top model to the one in the photograph, or even larger. I used a large box of double-thickness corrugated cardboard. For smaller totem poles, you can use a box made of single-thickness cardboard.

Totem pole made from the corners of a carton, 5 feet 2 inches high.

Top half of the totem pole in the photo on page 29. The three sections make an interesting design in themselves.

How to Make It

1. Decide on the approximate size you want for your totem pole sections. Then draw two lines an equal distance from one corner of the box as in Figure 1. These will mark the width of the sections. Do the same at another corner of the box if you need more sections.

2. Cut through these lines with your matt knife (Figure 2).

3. Then rule this corner strip into equal vertical sections (Figure 3). They should be slightly larger than the width you used.

4. Cut out the equal vertical sections (Figure 4).

5. Cut four slots into each section as shown in Figure 5.

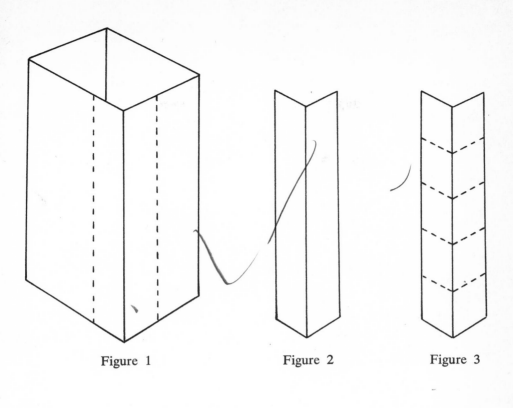

Figure 1   Figure 2   Figure 3

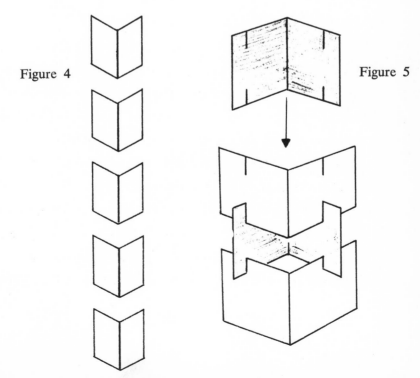

Figure 4   Figure 5

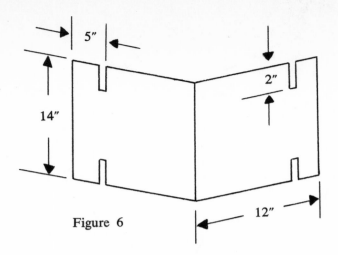

Figure 6

The slots must be in the same place on each section or they will not fit together. Figure 6 shows the size and position of the slots used for the totem pole in the photograph.
6. Now fit the sections together and glue them. Bend one section out, then the next section in, as shown in Figure 5. Use as many sections as you need to make your totem pole as high as you wish. You can slot in a beak or projection at the top if you want; see page 25.

Decorating
Figure 7 shows the design used in the totem pole in the photograph. You can refer to other photographs and drawings in the book for designs, or invent your own.

Since the cardboard I used was brown and had no printing on it, I left it unpainted. I cut the large sections of the design from black paper and glued them on. The thinner lines were painted with black acrylic paint. This gave the appearance of natural wood with a carved design.

You may choose to paint your entire totem pole. You

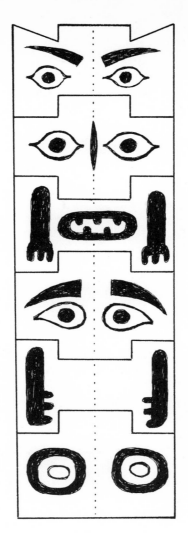

Figure 7

can use any colors you like. However, black or dark outlines will make the design stand out better.

Making a Base

You may want a base for your totem pole so it will be less likely to fall over. For a 3-foot or smaller pole, glue a flat piece of cardboard to the bottom. For a larger pole, screw a 1 x 1-inch length of wood to a plywood base as shown in Figure 8; a lumberyard will cut the wood to size. The wood is held to the base with angle brackets. You can tie the totem pole to the wood strip as shown in Figure 9.

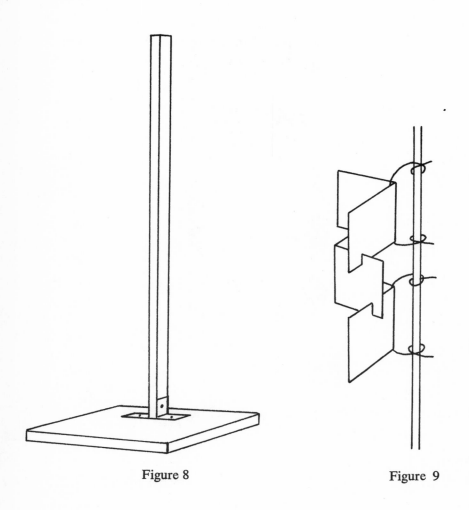

Figure 8   Figure 9

Saltbox House

Like the Indians, the early Colonial settlers built their houses by hand. The frames were fitted together with wooden joints and held together with wooden pegs. Nails, which had to be made one at a time by a blacksmith, were too expensive to use.

The saltbox house was a popular architectural style. According to the New York Historical Association, this design was nicknamed "saltbox" because it resembled the boxes colonists kept in their pantries for storing salt.

The Conklin saltbox house. You can see where the shed-type addition is attached to the main section of the house.

PHOTOGRAPHED AT OLD BETHPAGE VILLAGE RESTORATION.

Another view of the Conklin house. Notice that the addition does not extend the full width of the house.

PHOTOGRAPHED AT OLD BETHPAGE VILLAGE RESTORATION.

Cardboard saltbox house, 2 feet by 1½ feet, 15 inches high.

MADE BY REGINA KELHETTER (S).

A typical saltbox house started with a simple basic design as shown in Figure 1. As the family's needs grew, rooms were added. The frames could be unpegged to attach the additions. A common way of enlarging a house was to add a shed-type room with a sloping roof. The slope of the roof could be at a different angle from that of the main roof (Figure 2) or the angle could be the same (Figure 3). Many houses were designed with saltbox-style additions from the beginning.

Some barns were also built in the saltbox style. The longer sloping roof faced north and the higher portion faced the warm south. The saltbox design stands as a classic of early American architecture.

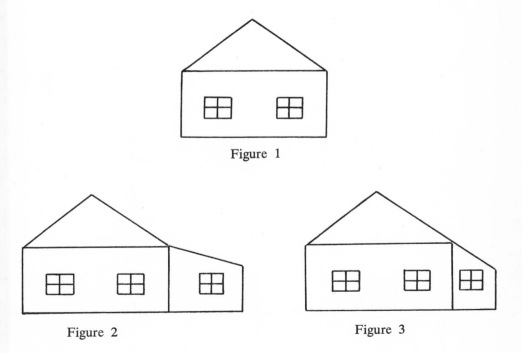

Figure 1

Figure 2   Figure 3

Materials

basic tools, *plus*

2 corrugated cardboard boxes, one 12 inches square or larger and the other somewhat smaller (If you want the addition to extend the full width of the main house, the boxes should measure the same in one direction.)

single-thickness corrugated cardboard, about 13 x 30 inches

water-base paint, white or brick red

acrylic paint, black and white

½-inch paintbrush

#2 pointed watercolor brush

How to Make It

1. Place the boxes side by side in a clear work area (Figure 4). You will make the main section of the house from box 1. Box 2 will be used for the sloping addition.

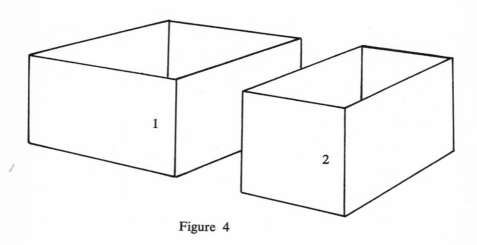

Figure 4

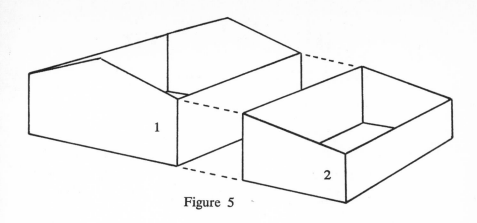

Figure 5

2. Lay out and cut the sloping roof as in Figure 5. Follow the procedure outlined on page 22 for building the Haida house. Make sure the inner wall of box 2 will reach the roof of box 1.

You can make either a one-story or a two-story house. If you decide on two stories, make the angle of the roof of the main section steeper and cut down the addition to make it lower.

3. Glue box 1 to box 2.

4. Cut and glue on the roof, following the method outlined on page 23.

5. Paint the house with two thin coats of white or brick red paint. Draw the boards, windows, and doors lightly with pencil. Paint the windows white. When they are dry, paint the window frames, the door, and the lines of the boards with black paint.

Colonial Barn

The design and construction of the Colonial barn has become a classic of American architecture. In most cases the massive beams were cut at least a year before the barn was to be erected so they would have time to season. The frame was held together with interlocking wooden joints and the sides were covered with heavy boards. The door hinges were hand-forged by a blacksmith and attached with heavy handmade nails. The door latches were made of wood.

Barn with fenced-in area for horses.

PHOTOGRAPHED AT OLD BETHPAGE VILLAGE RESTORATION.

TOP: *Interlocking timbers were used to make the fence.*

CENTER: *Hand-forged hinges were held in place with heavy nails. The nails and hinges were made by the blacksmith.*

BOTTOM: *Many barns were signed and dated by their builders. This massive roof support is carved with the initials HW and dated 1841.*

PHOTOGRAPHED AT OLD BETHPAGE VILLAGE RESTORATION.

The barn door is held in place by a sliding wooden latch. Here the latch is pulled back so that the door can swing open.

PHOTOGRAPHED AT OLD BETHPAGE VILLAGE RESTORATION.

Aged wooden barn siding has a rich texture and color.

The beauty of a barn made almost 150 years ago is still inspiring. Its aged wood has turned a rich gray color with a deep raised grain brought out by years of exposure to the weather. The wood from old barns is highly prized today. It is used to make rustic picture frames and to add antique touches to modern interiors.

Your cardboard barn will be large enough to use as a playhouse. However, since you will be using a refrigerator carton, it will not have the same proportions as a real barn;

Cardboard barn with a latched window. The barn is 4½ feet high.

it will be taller in proportion to its length. You could make a small toy barn with the same proportions as a real barn if you wish.

Materials
basic tools, *plus*
large corrugated box used to ship a refrigerator
    (These boxes are about 5 feet high and 3 feet square. The bottom is constructed with extra strength. I have seen these boxes outside houses after refrigerators were delivered. My neighbor was happy to give me one, since it is a hard item to dispose of.)
double-thickness or laminated corrugated cardboard, about 12 inches square
1-inch wide gauze strip, about 12 inches long
water-base paint, gray or red
acrylic paint, black
½-inch paintbrush

How to Make It
1. Set the box upright in a large clear work area (Figure 1). You will need to be able to walk around it as you work.
2. Unlike those of the other houses, the roof of the barn is made from the box itself rather than from a separate piece. This stronger method of construction is needed because of the barn's large size.
3. Find the center of one side of the house and cut at an

angle for the roof as you did for the Haida house and saltbox house (Figure 2). Cut the opposite side the same way.

Make sure you cut down far enough so that the side of
the roof section (A) is as long as or a little longer than
the sloping edge (B).

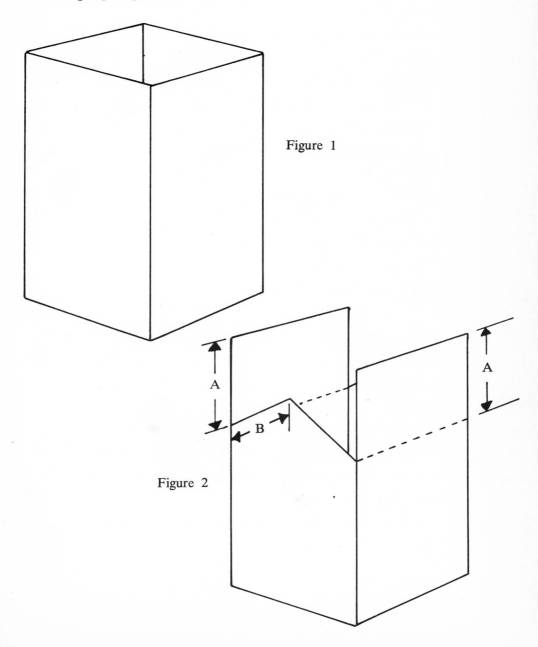

Figure 1

Figure 2

You may have to stand on a stool or box to work on the barn's roof. Don't try to turn the box on its side, because the pressure of your knife may cave the box in.

4. With your matt knife, score along the dotted lines (Figure 3) and bend the roof sections down. Trim the ends of the roof sections if necessary so that they meet at the top. Glue the roof down and tape it in position with masking tape. Let the glue dry overnight. Remove the tape and smear a little glue into any areas roughened by the tape.

5. Cut an opening large enough so you can enter the barn. Remember, the larger the opening, the weaker the box will become, so try to keep the doorway as small as possible (Figure 4).

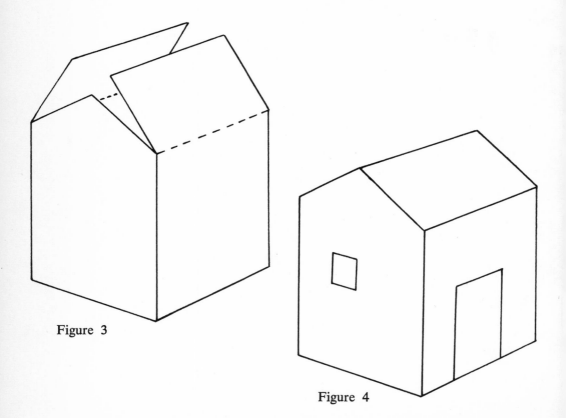

Figure 3

Figure 4

Cardboard barn latch made of double-thickness cardboard.

The window is unlatched in order to open.

A real barn would have a door to open and close, but the cardboard is not strong enough to support a door.

6. For a barn made from a refrigerator carton, make the hinged window about 9 by 7 inches. A larger one might cause structural problems. Cut a 9 x 7-inch hole in one side of the barn (Figure 4). Cut four pieces of the gauze strip

47

and glue them to the window shutter and barn wall to act as hinges (Figure 5).

7. Cut three brackets and one slide bar from double-thickness or laminated cardboard as shown in Figure 6. The proportions indicated are for a 9 x 7-inch window.

8. Rule a line (the dotted line in Figure 7) across the shutter and the barn wall. Trace around each bracket end to see where to make the slots. Make sure the brackets are positioned close enough together to hold the slide bar—see the photo on page 47.

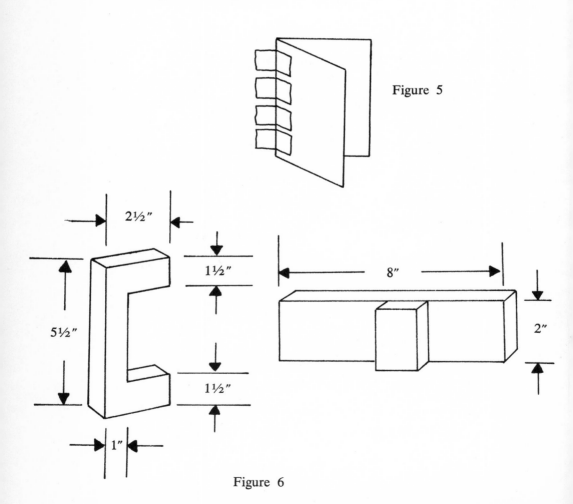

Figure 5

Figure 6

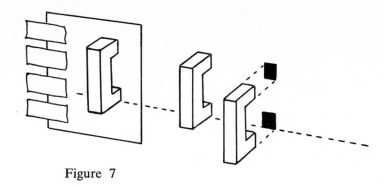

Figure 7

9. Cut out the slots and glue in the brackets. Take care not to push the brackets too far in. The slide must be able to go through them easily.

10. If you want, cut an open window (without a hinged shutter) in the other wall of the barn to let in light.

11. Many Colonial barns were painted red. However, the one in the photograph was painted with gray water-base paint to look like weathered wood. The boards and roof shingles were painted with black acrylic paint and a "dry brush." This means that very little water is used so the painted lines have a rough look. The hinges were painted with diluted black acrylic paint.

Variations

Other latch and hinge styles are shown in the source material chapter. You might want to add another hinged window to your barn.

Another interesting project would be to make a smaller barn with an operating door or window on each side. This would be a good toy for a small child.

49

Well

The Colonial settlers did not have piped-in water in their homes as we do. They had to dig a hole deep enough to reach the water level. Then a well structure was built over the hole to hold a bucket and crank for bringing up the water.

Stone and wood well.

Cardboard well, 6 inches high, with operating crank.

MADE BY DAVID ROSENTHAL (S).

The top structures of many wells are now used as decorations for lawns or backyards. Small replicas are often used as planters. Wells are interesting to look at and they are also a link with our Colonial past.

Materials

basic tools, *plus*

round 26-ounce salt box (You can also use the cardboard core from a roll of wrapping twine.)

¼ x ¼-inch balsa wood strip, 12 inches long (available in hobby shops)

⅛-inch diameter dowel rod, 12 inches long (available in hobby shops) cardboard cylinder from aluminum foil

thin cardboard from a cereal box

button cord (heavy sewing cord)

acrylic paint—black and white, or colors of your choice

#2 pointed watercolor brush

compass

How to Make It

1. Cut down the salt container so it is about 3 inches high. Rub glue into any rough edges and any spots where the label is peeling.

2. Cut two 6-inch lengths of the balsa strip and glue them upright in the bottom of the container. Make sure the two strips are opposite one another (Figure 1).

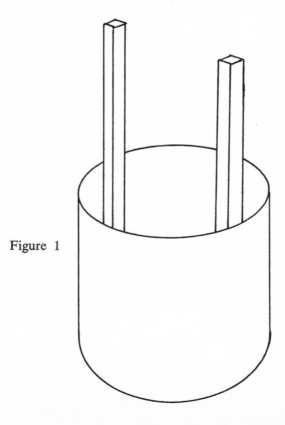

Figure 1

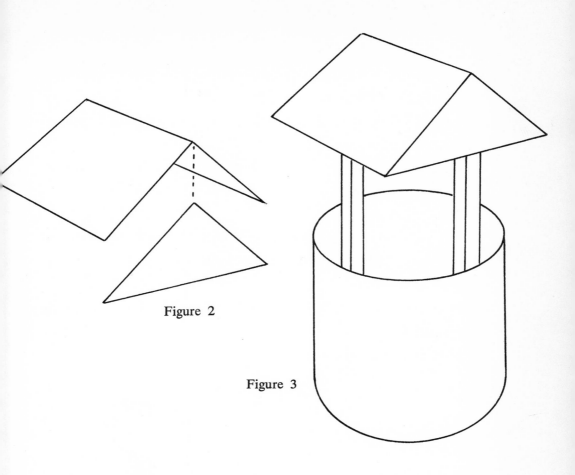

Figure 2

Figure 3

3. From the cereal-box cardboard, make a roof that will fit over the wood uprights. Bend the cardboard over the edge of a ruler to make a straight fold. Then cut out and glue two triangles at the ends (Figure 2). Use masking tape to hold the roof together while it dries.

Glue the roof to the uprights (Figure 3).

4. Cut a 1-inch length of the cardboard cylinder to make the bucket. Trace around the end of the cylinder on the cereal-box cardboard. Cut out this circle and glue it to

the bottom of the 1-inch cylinder (Figure 4). With the point of the compass, push two holes in the bucket and attach the button cord as shown.

5. The crank is shown in Figure 5. Cut an oval (A) about 1 inch long from thin cardboard. Make two holes in it with the compass point; the holes should be about ⅛ inch in diameter and they should not be too close to the edge of the oval.

Cut a piece of the dowel stick a little longer than the width of the roof and another shorter piece about 1½ inches long. Glue them into the holes in the cardboard oval as shown (B).

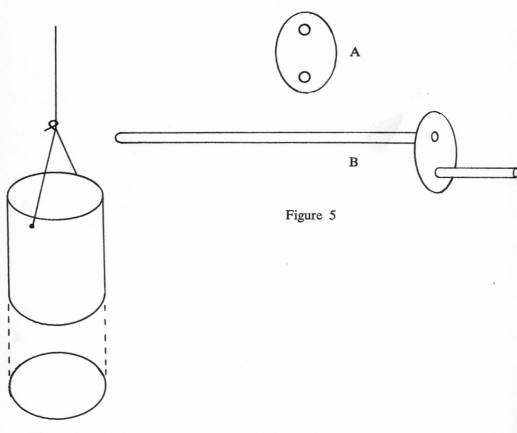

Figure 5

Figure 4

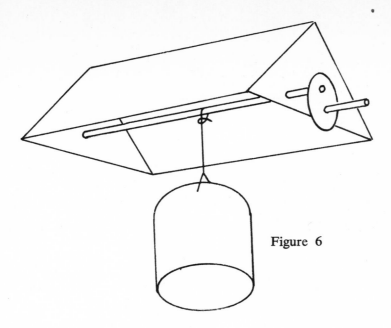

Figure 6

6. Figure 6 shows the crank and bucket set into the roof. The long dowel is inserted through two holes in the sides of the roof. The cord from the bucket is tied and glued to the dowel; the glue will keep the cord from slipping as you turn the crank.

You can make larger or smaller wells, depending on the size of the cylinder you start with. Just keep in mind that as the well becomes larger, the upright supports must be taller.

7. The well in the photograph was painted to simulate a stone bottom and wooden roof. Be sure to dilute the acrylic paint so it flows on smoothly without streaking.

Kachina Dolls

In religious dance ceremonies of the Hopi Indians, masked male dancers impersonate the Kachina spirits. The wooden Kachina dolls made by the Hopi represent these

LEFT: *Kachina doll, Hopi Indians.*   COURTESY OF THE BROOKLYN MUSEUM.

RIGHT: *Kachina doll, Hopi Indians.*

COLLECTION OF MR. AND MRS. HARRY COMINS.

masked dancers. The dolls are given to children to help them learn about the Kachinas, as part of their religious training. They are not considered toys, nor are they worshipped. The dolls are hung from walls and rafters where they can be seen at all times. There seem to be more than two hundred Kachinas, and the costume of the same Kachina varies from village to village.

Your cardboard Kachina doll will not duplicate a particular Hopi Kachina. The dolls shown here combine elements from different Indian designs. You can construct

LEFT: *Kachina-inspired doll made from cardboard, felt, and feathers. One blue bead adds a colorful accent.*

RIGHT: *Kachina-inspired cardboard doll with glass bead necklace.*

Kachina-inspired cardboard doll. Large colored feathers and wooden beads make this doll very striking. MADE BY ELAINA HOLOWATY (S).

your own variation of a Kachina doll. Consult the photographs and drawings in this book for ideas.

Your doll's mask will be made from 1½-inch diameter cardboard tube. The dimensions suggested for the body will keep your doll in proportion. If you start with a larger tube, you can increase the overall size of your doll.

58

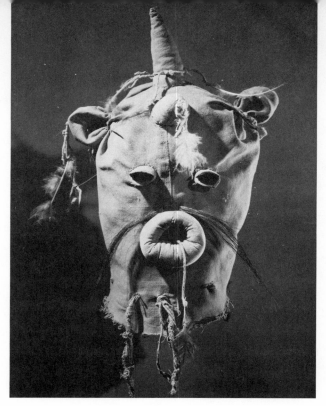

These three Kachina masks from Hopi dance ceremonies show some of the variations in design. ABOVE: *Tacheukti (clown) Kachina*. BELOW LEFT: *Tacab Kachina*. BELOW RIGHT: *Huo (bear) Kachina*.

Materials

basic tools, *plus*

cardboard cylinder from aluminum foil, 1½-inch diameter

thin cardboard from a cereal box

single-thickness corrugated cardboard, about 9 x 12 inches

thumbtack

acrylic paints, colors of your choice

small pointed paintbrush

2 small feathers

beads ⎤

thread ⎬ optional

felt scraps ⎦

How to Make It

1. Cut a 2-inch length of the cardboard tube and glue on a top cut from cereal-box cardboard (Figure 1). Glue the printed side face down so it won't show. This is the main section of the doll's mask.

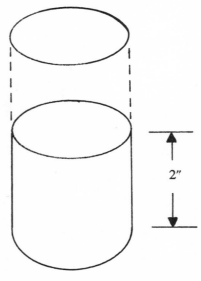

2"

Figure 1

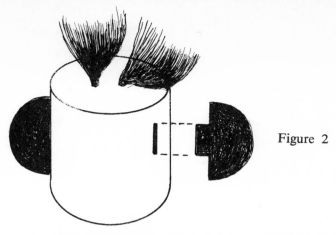

Figure 2

2. Cut thin slots in the sides of the mask. Then cut out two ears from thin cardboard and glue them in the slots (Figure 2).

3. Draw the body and arms on the corrugated cardboard and cut them out with your X-acto knife (Figure 3). Notice how the top of the body is designed to fit into the mask.

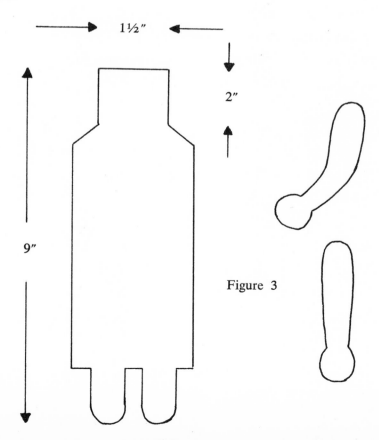

1½"

2"

9"

Figure 3

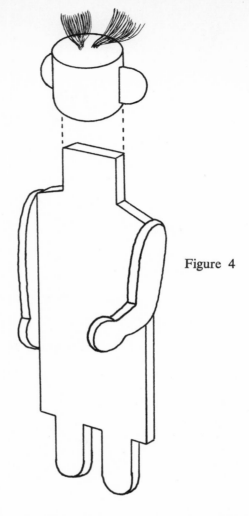

Figure 4

4. Glue the mask and arms in position (Figure 4).

5. Paint your doll with diluted acrylic paints. You can follow the design shown in the photograph if you wish; use a pinkish or light tan color for the skin, and whatever colors you wish for the mask, shorts, and moccasins.

Punch two small holes in the top with the point of the tack and glue in the feathers. A rattle or stick can be attached with thread through a hole punched in the hand.

6. Figure 5 shows another type of mask made from the same size cardboard tube as the mask in Figure 1. Figure 6 shows the mask attached to a flat body the same size as the one in Figure 3. This time the arms are not made separately from the body.

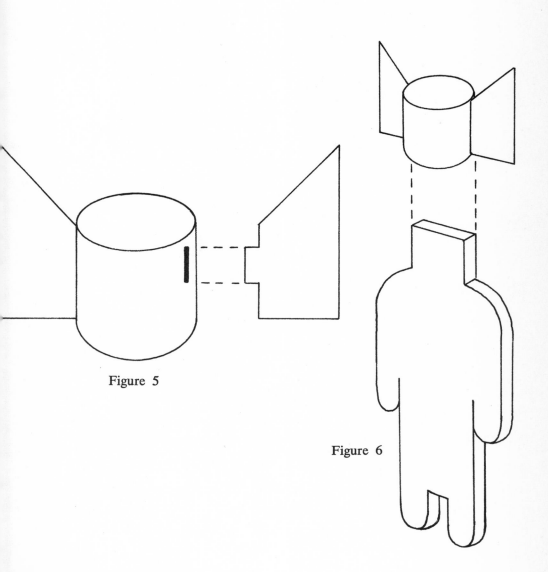

Figure 5

Figure 6

Paint your dolls in whatever colors you wish, and add beads or scraps of felt to their costumes. Figure 7 will give you some ideas for designing the mask.

Figure 7

Decoys

Both the Indians and the Colonial settlers made life-size duck decoys. A group of decoys was floated on the water to attract water fowl and bring them into the hunter's range. The Indians made realistic decoys from tied rush covered with feathers. The Colonial settlers carved decoys from wood and then painted them.

Unfinished rush duck decoy, Lovelock Cave, Nevada.
PHOTOGRAPH COURTESY OF MUSEUM OF THE AMERICAN INDIAN, HEYE FOUNDATION.

14-inch duck decoy made of tule rush, over which is spread a duck's skin. Paviotso-Paiute, Stillwater, Nevada.

PHOTOGRAPH COURTESY OF MUSEUM OF THE AMERICAN INDIAN, HEYE FOUNDATION.

Early American wooden duck decoy painted black and white.

COLLECTION OF THE AUTHOR.

*Detail of wooden decoy, showing glass eye. The head is carved from a
separate wood block and pegged onto the body.*

*Workshop where duck decoys and fishing gear were made. This workshop
is the addition to the Conklin saltbox house on pages 35 and 36.*

Many early decoys had the artistic qualities of sculpture. Although most hunters now use mass-produced decoys, artists continue to carve decoys as an art form. There are also modern wicker birds whose decorative qualities are similar to those of the uncovered Indian rush decoys.

You can make a cardboard duck decoy which will capture the feeling of the early American ones.

Carved walnut sculpture of a curlew, inspired by the simple lines of shore bird decoys. The long beak is set into a hole in the head.

MADE BY THE AUTHOR.

Cardboard duck decoy.

Cardboard duck decoy covered with feathers.

Materials

basic tools, *plus*

cardboard cylinder from aluminum foil, 1½-inch diameter

thin cardboard from a cereal box

acrylic paint, black and white

small paintbrush

feathers (optional)

How to Make It

1. Cut a 4-inch length of cardboard tube (Figure 1). This size will keep the bird's length in proportion to the 1½-inch diameter of the tube. If you have a larger tube, you can increase the bird's length.

2. Cut one end of the tube up at an angle (Figure 2).

3. Draw the shape of the head on thin cardboard and cut it out (Figure 3). Notice the projection behind the bird's neck to make it fit snugly into the tube.

If you are making a larger decoy, use corrugated cardboard for the head and tail.

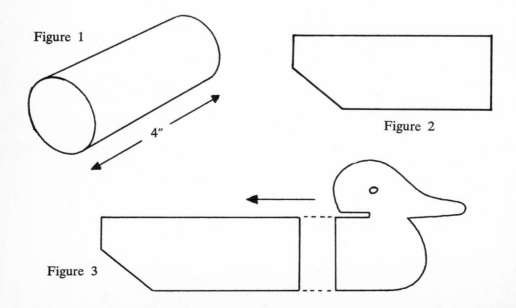

Figure 1

4"

Figure 2

Figure 3

4. Figure 4 shows the shape of the tail. Make it 2 inches long so that 1 inch fits into the tube.

5. Insert and glue the head and tail in the body as shown in Figure 5. Also glue a small square of thin cardboard on the bottom to serve as a base.

6. Cut out two wing shapes (Figure 6). Bend the front of each wing as shown in Figure 7.

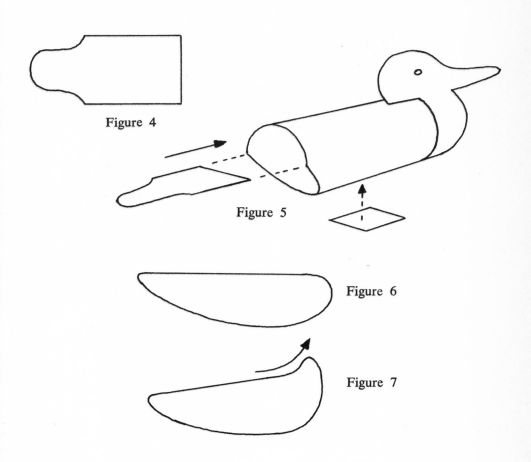

Figure 4

Figure 5

Figure 6

Figure 7

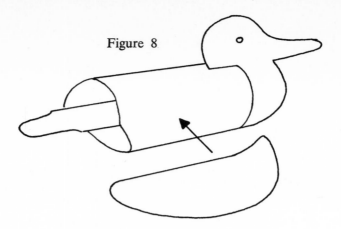

Figure 8

7. Glue the wings to the sides of the bird (Figure 8).
8. The bird is painted with diluted black acrylic paint; the wings and eyes are white. If you are making a feathered decoy, glue the feathers over the surface after it is painted. You can also try varying the shape of the decoy's head and wings, as shown in Figure 9.

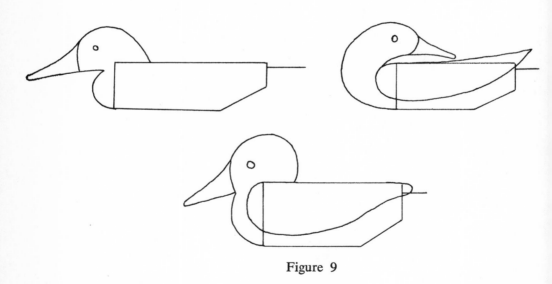

Figure 9

SHORE BIRD DECOYS

The Colonial settlers hunted shore birds as well as ducks, so they needed another type of decoy to stand in the reeds at the water's edge. The shore bird decoy is made the same way as the duck decoy, except that the body is supported on a stand. Since these birds have very long beaks, you will carve one from a matchstick.

Cardboard shore bird decoy. The beak is carved from a matchstick.

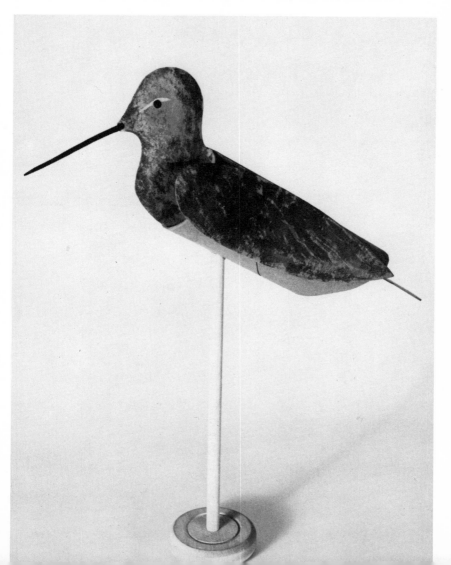

How to Make It

1. Use a 5-inch length of tube for the shore bird's body. Construct it the same way you made the duck decoy. Notice, however, the change in the angle of the head (Figure 10).

2. The stand is made from a ¼-inch dowel or a stick from a Tinker Toy set. The stick is inserted in a hole in the bottom of the tube. Make the hole with the point of a scissors. Glue the stick in place and attach it to a Tinker Toy disk as a base (Figure 11). If a Tinker Toy part is not available, use a scrap of wood with a hole drilled in it.

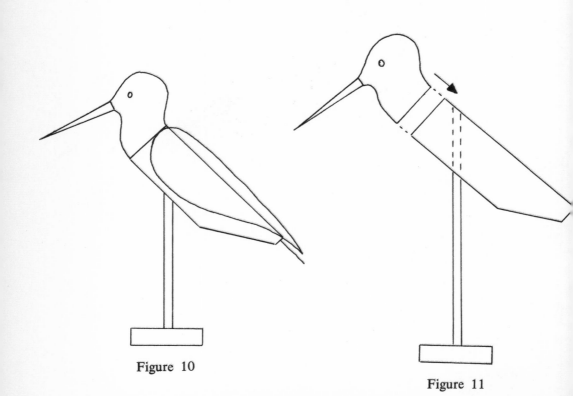

Figure 10

Figure 11

Figure 12

3. Whittle the beak from a matchstick. Insert it in a small slot in the bird's head (Figure 12).

4. Shore bird decoys have a speckled appearance, as seen in the photograph. Mix several shades of gray acrylic paint from different proportions of black and white. Dab the various shades on to give a speckled look. Paint the beak and the eye in black and white.

Rocking Horse

Wooden rocking horses were popular toys for Colonial children. Because they were carved and constructed by hand, many of them had beautiful sculptural qualities.

Your cardboard rocking horse will not be strong enough to sit on, but the rocking action will be quite realistic.

Early American rocking horse.
THE ELEANOR AND MABEL VAN ALSTYNE AMERICAN FOLK ART COLLECTION. SMITHSONIAN INSTITUTION.

Rocking horse, 42 inches long and 24 inches high.

Cardboard rocking horse, 24 inches long and 24 inches high, with a tail made of twine.　　　　MADE BY NICHOLAS PUCCIA (S).

Materials

basic tools, *plus*

oblong cardboard box, 12 to 20 inches long

3 pieces of double-thickness or laminated corrugated cardboard, a few inches longer than the box

single-thickness corrugated cardboard, about 15 inches square

string or twine

acrylic or water-base paint, colors of your choice

paintbrush

How to Make It

1. Glue all the box's seams together (Figure 1). Use masking tape to hold them while the glue dries. This will create a strong body for the horse.

2. Draw the head on the single-thickness corrugated cardboard. Cut it out with the matt knife and glue it to the front of the box (Figure 2). For added strength, you can insert the head into a slot in the box.

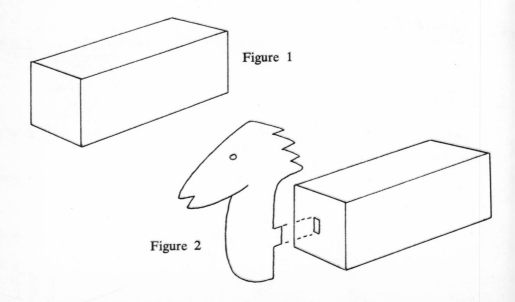

Figure 1

Figure 2

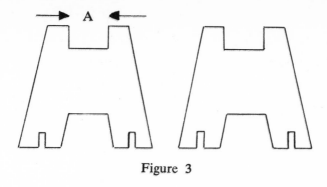

Figure 3

Figure 4

3. Cut two sets of legs, as shown in Figure 3. These are made from double-thickness or laminated corrugated cardboard. The cut-out section "A" should fit tightly around the box.

4. Cut two rockers from double-thickness or laminated corrugated cardboard, as shown in Figure 4. You can experiment with different sizes and curves; however, the rockers should not be more than 28 inches long, or they will not be strong enough.

5. Glue the horse together as shown in Figure 5. Cut a hole in the back of the box and glue in strands of twine for the tail.

6. Paint the horse with any colors you choose; it can look realistic or fanciful.

Figure 5

Trestle Table

The Colonial settlers constructed a type of simple and strong table called a "trestle table." The feature that makes it unique is a single crossbeam which connects the legs. This crossbeam is held in place with pegs.

You can build a cardboard game table in the style of a trestle table. Don't try to make it larger than the directions indicate, however, because the cardboard will not be strong enough.

Trestle table with constructed legs. Notice the crossbeam and peg.
PHOTOGRAPHED BY COLONIAL WILLIAMSBURG.

Trestle tables and other early American objects can often be found in shops throughout the country.   COBWEB CORNER, SPARTA, N.J.

Cardboard trestle table.

Detail of trestle table made of laminated cardboard. The crossbeam is placed at the top of the legs to support the table top.

Trestle table, 2 inches high, made from ⅛-inch thick wood. It can be used as a miniature plant stand or in a dollhouse.

Popular trestle table style with solid legs and pegged crossbeam.

Materials

basic tools, *plus*

double-thickness or laminated corrugated cardboard, about 30 inches square (Double thickness is essential for a table this size.)

2 wooden pegs, about 1½ inches long (These can be cut from ½-inch diameter twigs or wood strips from a lumberyard.)

water-base paint, any color

paintbrush

How to Make It

1. On the double-thickness cardboard, rule out in pencil the four pieces needed for the table (Figure 1). Cut the pieces out with the matt knife. The slots in the legs should be as wide as the thickness of the cardboard so the brace will fit snugly.

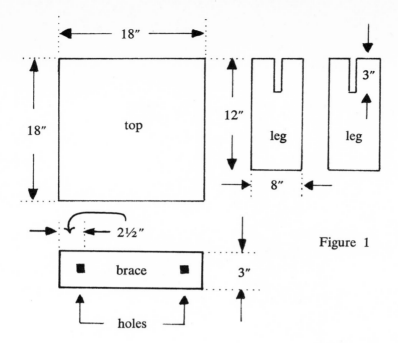

Figure 1

Cut holes in the brace the same diameter as the pegs so they will fit tightly.

2. Glue the table together as shown in Figure 2. Be sure that the legs are straight and the top is centered. Check to see that the peg holes are outside the legs.

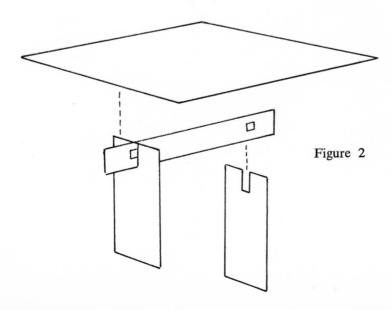

Figure 2

3. Insert the pegs as shown in Figure 3 and glue them in place.

4. Paint the table any color you wish, or use a combination of colors.

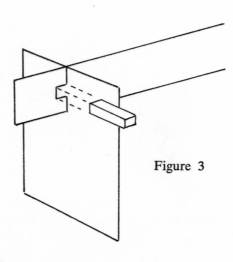

Figure 3

Cradle

The Colonial settlers made beautiful wooden cradles. Unlike many modern cradles, they were built close to the ground. Their simple lines lend themselves easily to cardboard construction.

Early American wooden cradle.   PHOTOGRAPHED BY COLONIAL WILLIAMSBURG.

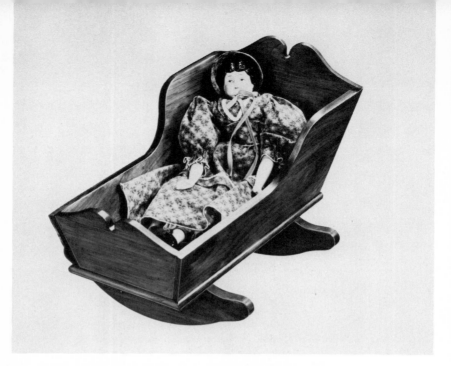

Modern copy of early American cradle, with uncovered top.

Early American cradle. Notice the graceful rockers and slatted bottom.

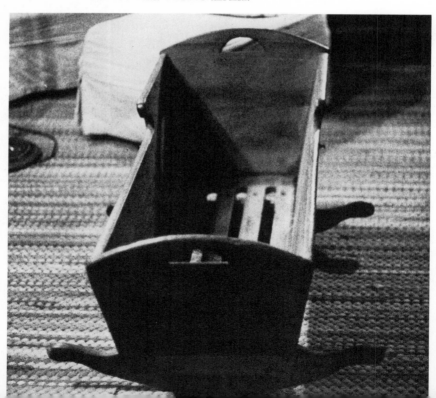

Cardboard cradle constructed from a box 14 inches long and 10 inches wide.

The cradle in the photo is large enough for a doll and blanket. It is 14 inches long and 10 inches wide. You can make a cradle this size or use a very small box that will fit in a dollhouse.

Materials
basic tools, *plus*
cardboard box, up to 14 inches long
double-thickness or laminated corrugated cardboard, about 12 x 14 inches
single-thickness corrugated cardboard, about 5 x 10 inches
acrylic or water-base paint, any color you wish
paintbrush

How to Make It

1. Draw the outline of the cradle body on the box (Figure 1) and cut it out.

2. Cut the roof with the matt knife from single-thickness cardboard. Glue it to the cradle body as shown in Figure 2. Use masking tape to hold it in place while the glue dries. (If you prefer, you can make a cradle without a roof, as shown in the photographs.)

Figure 3 shows the completed cradle body.

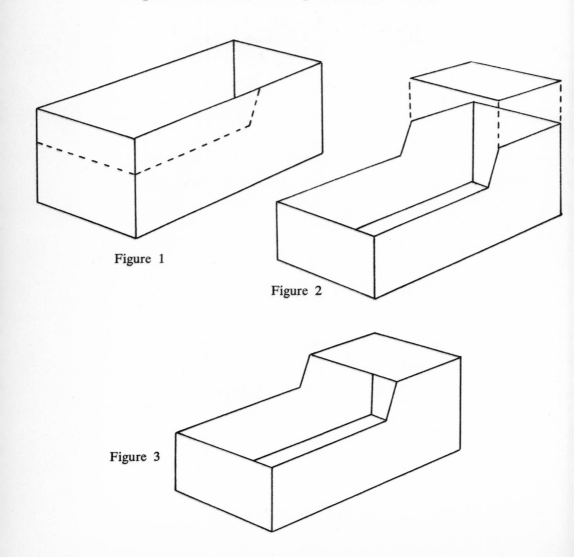

Figure 1

Figure 2

Figure 3

Figure 4   Figure 5

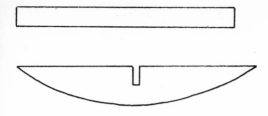

3. Cut two rockers and a brace from double-thickness or laminated corrugated cardboard (Figure 4). (If your cradle is less than 8 inches long, you can use single-thickness cardboard for the rockers and brace.) Cut a slot in each rocker so that the brace will fit all the way in.

4. Glue the rockers onto the brace (Figure 5). Then glue the rockers and brace to the bottom of the cradle. The rockers can be held in place with tape while the glue dries.

5. Colonial cradles were made of natural wood. If you want yours to have a similar look, use light yellow-brown or brown paint. Or paint the cradle in your own choice of colors.

Cart

A variety of wagons and carts were used on Colonial farms. They were pulled by horses or oxen and were used to transport crops and goods of all sorts. The cardboard cart you will make is a typical Colonial design.

Colonial wooden cart. PHOTOGRAPHED AT OLD BETHPAGE VILLAGE RESTORATION.

Cart made from a 12-inch square carton. The 10-inch diameter wheels are made from double-thickness cardboard.

Materials

basic tools, *plus*

strong corrugated box, about 12 inches long (The kind used to package small appliances like toasters or radios is best.)

single-thickness corrugated cardboard, about 9 x 15 inches

2 pieces of double-thickness or laminated corrugated cardboard, about 12 inches square

½-inch or ¼-inch square wood strip, 15 inches long (from a lumberyard)

¼-inch dowel stick, 12 inches long

water-base paint, any color

acrylic paint, black and white or colors of your choice

2 Tinker Toy disks, if available

thumbtack and string

How to Make It

1. Cut a ⅜-inch square hole at the bottom center of each side of the box (Figure 1).

2. Cut two single-thickness cardboard rectangles with ⅜-inch square cutouts as shown in Figure 2.

3. Glue these rectangles around the holes on the inside of the box (Figure 3). This will help support the cart's axle.

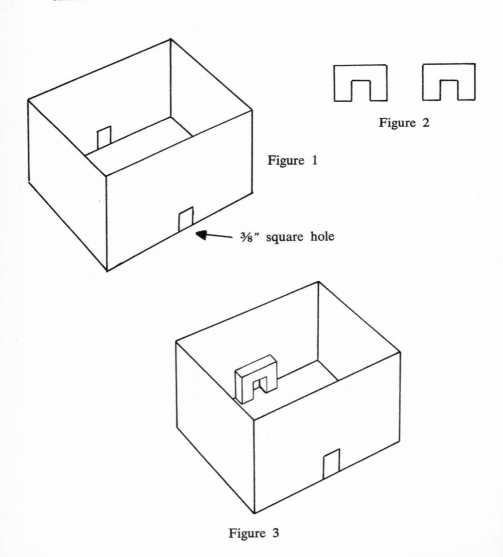

Figure 2

Figure 1

⅜" square hole

Figure 3

4. Make the front extension of the cart from single-thickness corrugated cardboard. The length of the extension should be equal to the length of the box, plus a few more inches to be glued under the box (Figure 4).

Figure 5 shows the extension glued in place.

5. It is best to use double-thickness corrugated cardboard for the wheels, so they will be sturdy. Cart wheels are usually quite large. The cart in the photograph has a 12-inch body and 10-inch diameter wheels.

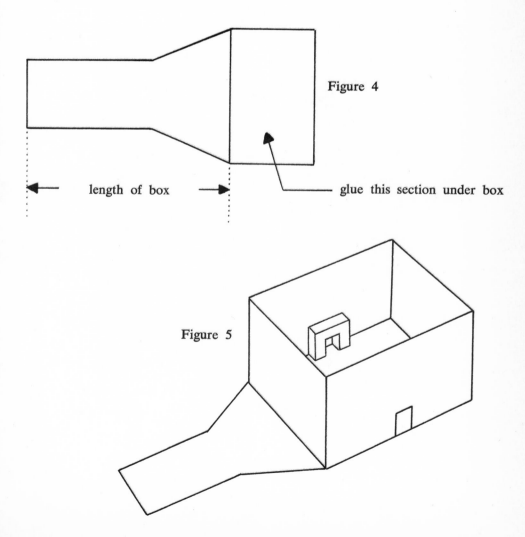

Figure 4

length of box

glue this section under box

Figure 5

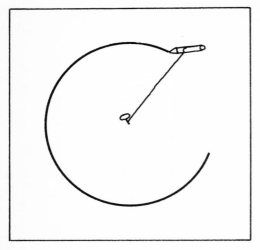
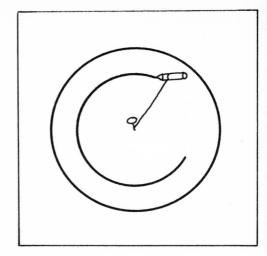

Figure 6   Figure 7

To make a wheel, push a thumbtack into the center of
one piece of double-thickness cardboard. Tie a string to
the thumbtack and stretch the string out to the distance
you want for the wheel's radius. Tie the string to a pencil
at this point. Holding the string taut, swing the pencil
around to draw the circle (Figure 6). (For smaller carts,
you can use a compass to make the wheels.)

To make the rim of the wheel, shorten the string and
swing the pencil around in the same way (Figure 7).

Draw another wheel in the same way and cut out both
wheels.

Painting and Assembling
6. Paint the body and the extension of the cart first. The
cart in the photograph was painted gray to look like
weathered wood.

96

7. The wheels can be painted with black and white acrylic paint, or whatever colors you wish. Paint the entire wheel first. When it is dry, paint on the rim and spokes in another color. The cart is now ready to assemble.

8. Glue the square wood strip under the full length of the extension, including the part under the cart (Figure 8).

9. Make a hole in the center of each wheel with the point of a scissors. Push the dowel through the wheels and through the holes in the cart body. Glue the wheels to the dowel, keeping the wheels close to the body. In this way, the wheels will turn with the axle, not individually.

10. Glue a Tinker Toy disk to each end of the dowel up against the wheel. This serves as a hub and gives strength to the wheel and axle assembly. If a Tinker Toy disk is not available, substitute a circle of corrugated cardboard with a hole in the center.

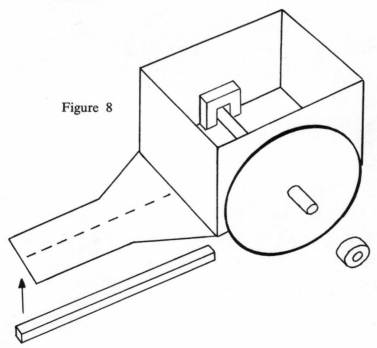

Figure 8

Covered Wagon

Covered wagons were the original mobile homes. The Colonial settlers lived in these wagons, sometimes called "prairie schooners," as they traveled west across the continent. The canvas cover shielded the travelers from rain and hot sun, and the wagon's body was large enough to carry household furniture and supplies for the journey.

Your cardboard covered wagon will be made in the same way as the cardboard cart.

Covered wagon. Notice the wood bracing on the wagon body. Some wagons were made of flat boards without bracing.

The strong wooden wheels are often used as garden decorations.

COBWEB CORNER, SPARTA, N.J.

Cardboard covered wagon with 8-inch body and 3-inch diameter wheels.

Materials

same materials as for cart, page 93, *plus*

2 more pieces of double-thickness or laminated corrugated
cardboard (for the second set of wheels)

1 more dowel stick (for the second axle)

1 sheet of white oaktag, about 12 x 20 inches

How to Make It

1. The body of the wagon is built like that of the cart.
You can cut the box down all the way around to make
a lower body. Make two sets of wheels instead of just one,
and make them a little smaller than the cart's wheels.

The wagon's front extension is about half the length of
the box (Figure 1). Compare this with Figure 8 on page
97 to see the difference. Add a small piece of cardboard
to the front of the wagon for a seat.

2. Paint the covered wagon before you assemble the
wheels, just as you did on the cart.

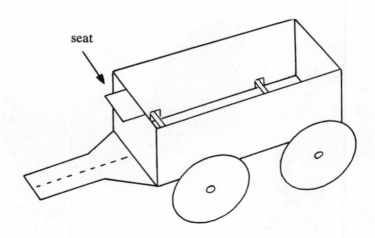

seat

Figure 1

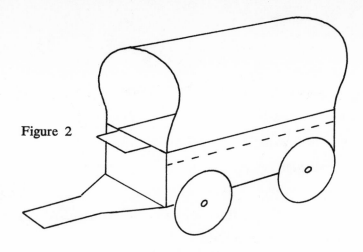

Figure 2

3. Cut a piece of white oaktag the length of the box. Bend it and glue it in place at the inner edges of the box (Figure 2). You can use masking tape on the inside of the box to hold the oaktag in place while the glue dries.

Leave the oaktag unpainted to resemble the cloth covering of the wagon.

Boxes

The Northwest Coast Indians who carved beautiful totem poles also decorated boxes and other objects in the same style. When designing flat objects, they spread out the design over the entire surface.

You can decorate a cardboard carton with a design derived from the Indian work. It will be a useful and decorative storage box for supplies or toys.

Carved and painted wooden box, 9½ inches high and 17 inches wide. Tlingit, Alaska.
PHOTOGRAPH COURTESY OF MUSEUM OF THE AMERICAN INDIAN, HEYE FOUNDATION.

Wooden food dish, Haida Indians. COURTESY OF THE BROOKLYN MUSEUM.

Tlingit ceremonial blanket. The designs used on this blanket can be incorporated in decorating your box.
COURTESY OF THE BROOKLYN MUSEUM.   BEQUEST OF DR. JAMES WATERMAN.

Decorated cardboard box, 24 inches long. The design can be applied with waterproof markers or paint.

Materials

basic tools, *plus*

strong cardboard box, any size (no printing on sides if possible)

black waterproof marker

light brown water-base paint and black acrylic paint (if box has printing)

How to Make It

1. You can leave the box the way you find it (Figure 1) or you can cut the sides in a curve as shown in Figure 2. To do this, first sketch the curve in pencil on each side. Then cut along the lines with the matt knife.

2. Figure 3 shows the design drawn on the box. The brown cardboard looked like wood and the design was sketched in pencil and filled in with a black marker. If your box has printing on it, you will have to paint it first

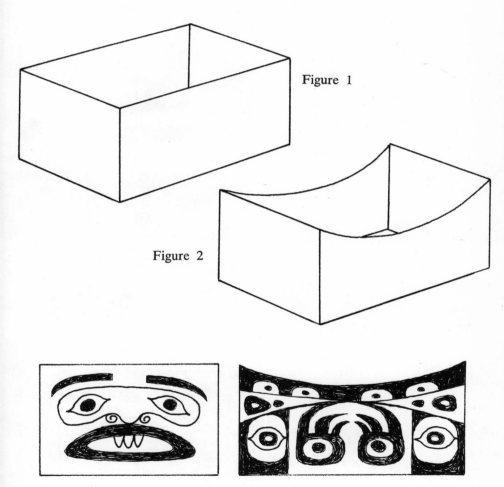

Figure 1

Figure 2

Figure 3

with light brown water-base paint. The design can then be sketched on in pencil. If the marker does not write on the paint, you can use diluted black acrylic paint and a small pointed brush to apply the design.

You can see that the Indian designs were repeated in a pattern. You can create your own design variation by first sketching different geometric patterns on the surface of the box (Figure 4). Then draw the design elements in your own arrangement. Figure 5 shows some Indian motifs that you can use in your own composition.

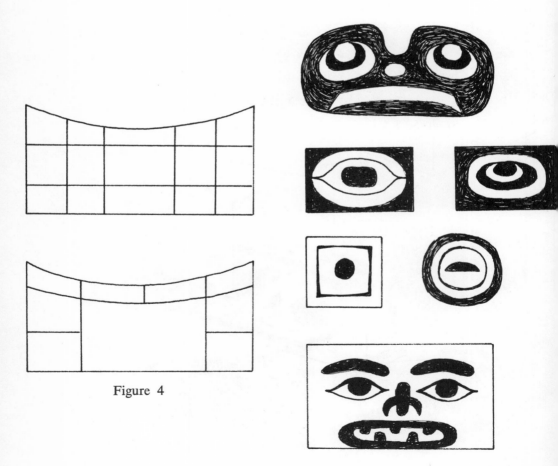

Figure 4

Figure 5

COLONIAL BOX

The Colonial settlers also made wooden boxes for storing things. Figure 6 shows one type of box they produced. Colonial boxes usually had a cover.

For a Colonial box, use a smallish sturdy cardboard box. Tape or glue the lid to make it solid if necessary, and use tape to reinforce the edge where the cover is attached.

You can also decorate a cigar box or an unfinished craft box in the Colonial style. Craft boxes can be obtained at hobby or art and craft supply stores. A wood box should be sandpapered lightly before you paint it.

You can copy the early American design below or refer to the source section and combine some of the motifs shown in your own way. Unlike the Northwest Coast Indian boxes, the Colonial designs do not fit within a geometric framework.

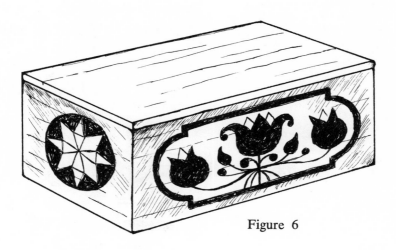

Figure 6

107

Source Material

The following pages provide drawings that will help you design your cardboard constructions. The latch and hinge styles will give you ideas for interesting variations on the basic barn design. The floral designs can be combined with the bird motifs for decorating cradles or boxes.

The photographs of Colonial buildings and objects in a blacksmith shop will expand the possibilities of the projects you make and give you a start on designing your own constructions.

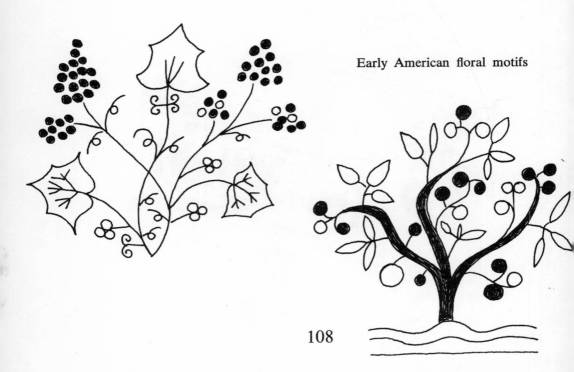

Early American floral motifs

108

Early American floral motifs

Birds from early American designs

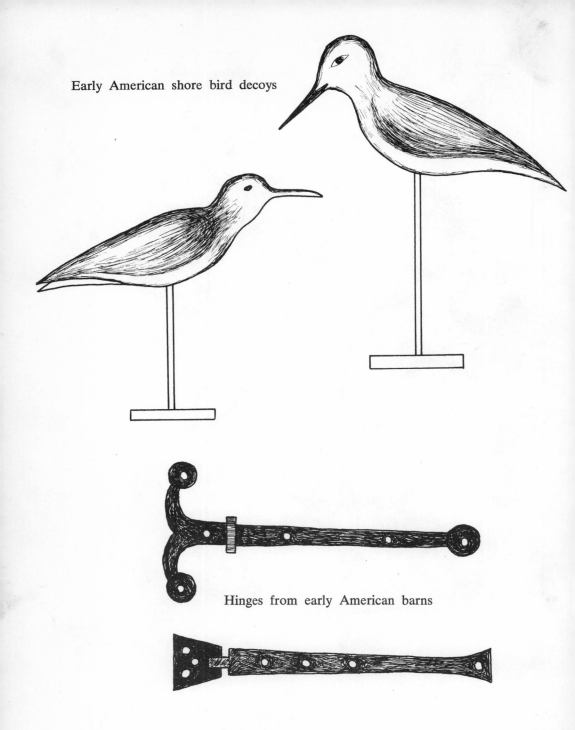

Early American shore bird decoys

Hinges from early American barns

110

Northwest Coast Indian house post

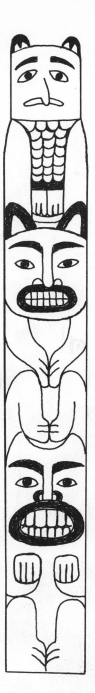

Northwest Coast Indian totem pole

Hopi Indian Kachina dolls

The fire in the blacksmith's forge must be kept stoked.

This modern-day blacksmith works in his shop with the same tools used by Colonial blacksmiths.

After the metal is heated in the forge, it is hammered to shape on this massive anvil. PHOTOGRAPHED AT OLD BETHPAGE VILLAGE RESTORATION.

Iron wheels were also made by Colonial blacksmiths.
PHOTOGRAPHED AT OLD BETHPAGE VILLAGE RESTORATION.

The walls of the shop are covered with various iron implements made by the blacksmith. PHOTOGRAPHED AT OLD BETHPAGE VILLAGE RESTORATION.

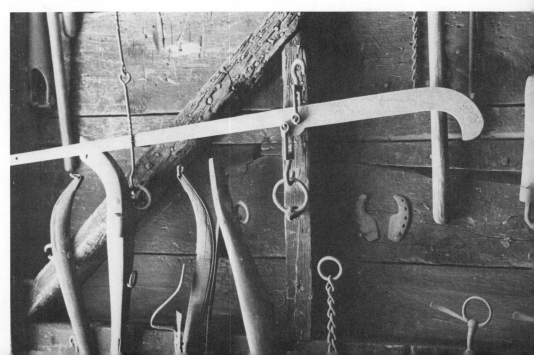

*Barn drop latch. The wooden bar drops into a notch in a wooden block.
The latch can be lifted from inside the barn with the cord.*
PHOTOGRAPHED AT OLD BETHPAGE VILLAGE RESTORATION.

*Wagon barn. You could make a cardboard barn like this to house your
cart or covered wagon.* PHOTOGRAPHED AT OLD BETHPAGE VILLAGE RESTORATION.

Colonial barn.   PHOTOGRAPHED AT OLD BETHPAGE VILLAGE RESTORATION.

Workbench and old hand tools. This area of the barn was used for carpentry and repair work. PHOTOGRAPHED AT OLD BETHPAGE VILLAGE RESTORATION.

Glossary

Acrylic paint: Plastic-base paint which can be diluted with water but which is waterproof when it dries.

Angle bracket: A fitting designed to brace a joint.

Anvil: A heavy, usually steel-faced, iron block on which hot metal is shaped by hand-hammering.

Balsa wood: A very lightweight wood which comes from South and Central America.

Blacksmith: A craftsman who shapes iron by heating and hammering it.

Brace: Support.

Bracket: A projecting support.

Cart: A two-wheeled conveyance without springs.

Corrugated cardboard: Three-layered paper board with a ridged central layer.

Craft: The use of skill and imagination in producing objects of beauty.

Dilute: To thin out.

Dowel: A round wooden stick.

Forged: Formed by heating and hammering (usually refers to metal).

Grain (of wood): The direction of the wood fibers.

Hinge: A jointed piece on which a door or gate turns or swings.

Homesote: A ridged board made from compressed cardboard which is used in building construction.

Laminated cardboard: Superimposed layers of cardboard glued together.

Latch: A device that holds something in place by sliding into a notch or opening.

Oaktag: Thin lightweight cardboard.

Peg: A small piece of wood used to fasten two pieces of material together.

Plywood: Board composed of sheets of thin wood cemented together.

Rush: A type of cylindrical grass with a hollow stem.

Score: To make a light cut in a material's surface so that it can be folded easily on the scored line.

Slot: A long narrow opening.

Metric Conversion Chart

———❖———

1 inch	=	2.54 centimeters or 25.4 millimeters
1 foot	=	0.30 meters
1 yard	=	0.91 meters

1 millimeter	=	0.04 inches
1 centimeter	=	0.39 inches
1 meter	=	39.37 inches, 3.3 feet, or 1.1 yards

The measurements used in this book are inches and feet. To convert to the metric system, round off the numbers as outlined in the following chart.

¼ inch	= 6 mm		4 inches	= 10 cm
⅜ inch	= 9 mm		10 inches	= 25 cm
½ inch	= 1¼ cm		1 foot	= 30 cm
1 inch	= 2½ cm		2 feet	= 60 cm
2 inches	= 5 cm		3 feet	= 90 cm
3 inches	= 7½ cm			

Suggested Reading

Many books about Indian and Colonial arts and crafts are available in libraries and bookstores. The following list includes books that came to my attention and that proved interesting and informative. You will probably find many others as you browse along the bookshelves.

Arthur, Eric, and Dudley Witney. *The Barn*. Toronto, Ontario: M. F. Feheley Arts Co., Ltd., 1972.

Claiborne, Robert, and Editors of Time-Life Books. *The First Americans*. New York: Time-Life Books, 1973.

Colton, Harold S. *Hopi Kachina Dolls*. Albuquerque, N.M.: The University of New Mexico Press, 1964.

Dockstader, Fredric J. *Indian Art in America: The Arts and Crafts of the American Indian*. New York: Promontory Press, n.d.

Feder, Norman. *American Indian Art* (shortened edition). New York: Harry N. Abrams, 1973.

Glubok, Shirley. *The Art of the Northwest Coast Indians*. New York: Macmillan Publishing Co., 1975.

Hass, Irvin. *America's Historic Villages and Restorations*. New York: Arco Publishing Co., 1974.

Hurst, Melvin J., and Elmer L. Smith. *Early Country Furniture*. Lebanon, Pa.: Applied Arts Publishers, 1970.

Shaker Furniture and Accessories. Concord, Mass.: Shaker Workshops, Inc., n.d.

Sloan, Eric. *An Age of Barns*. New York: Ballantine Books, 1974.

Smith, Elmer L. *American Wild Fowl Decoys from Folk Art to Factory*. Lebanon, Pa.: Applied Arts Publishers, 1970.

Webster, David S., and William Kehoe. *Decoys at Shelburne Museum*. Shelburne, Vt.: Shelburne Museum, 1961.

Wright, Barton. *This is a Hopi Kachina*. Flagstaff, Ariz.: Museum of Northern Arizona, 1965.

Magazine

Early American Life. Published by the Early American Society, P.O. Box 1831, Harrisburg, Pa. 17105 (monthly).

Craft Supply Sources

The tools and materials needed for your cardboard constructions are easy to find in most areas.

Plywood and homesote can be found in lumberyards and building supply stores; you can have them cut to the size you need.

Water-base paint and ½-inch or 1-inch wide paintbrushes for large areas are sold in paint stores, building supply stores, and lumberyards.

Metal rulers, matt knives, X-acto knives, masking tape, Elmer's glue, and wooden dowels are found in craft shops, art and stationery stores, and some paint stores, as well as in lumberyards and building supply stores.

For acrylic paints in tubes and fine paintbrushes for details, look in art stores, large stationery stores that carry art supplies, or art departments of department stores.

Extras such as beads, feathers, and felt are sold in craft shops.

If you have trouble finding any of the tools and supplies, or if you would like the convenience of ordering by mail, the following craft supply house will send you a complete catalog on request:

Vanguard Crafts
2915 Avenue J
Brooklyn, N.Y. 11210
(212) 377-5188

Index

ABOUT THE AUTHOR

Jeremy Comins is a teacher, artist and photographer. This book, which he hopes will stimulate an interest in both creative projects and American history, was an outgrowth of his project method of teaching art. Mr. Comins has had five one-man art exhibitions, and his work has been shown at the Museum of Modern Art, the Philadelphia Museum, and the Cooper Union Museum, among others. He and his wife live in Brooklyn, New York, with their two sons.